Inverse Thoughts

Inverse Thoughts

Mary;
Best of Luck
Spencer

Spencer

Library of Congress Control Number:		2011910345
ISBN:	Hardcover	978-1-4628-9176-4
	Softcover	978-1-4628-9175-7
	Ebook	978-1-4628-9177-1

This book was printed in the United States of America.

To order additional copies of this book, contact:
Xlibris Corporation
1-888-795-4274
www.Xlibris.com
Orders@Xlibris.com
100925

Dedication

To Susana, without whose encouragement these poems would still be scribbles on envelopes.

Contents

Late Snow

I saw a robin in the snow.
He wasn't happy there, I know.
He tried to make a little song.
It came out weak and sounded wrong.

I said to him, "You should migrate."
but he wouldn't leave his frozen mate.

I picked him up and brushed him off.
He responded with a little cough.
He moved a wing, but couldn't fly
and a little tear clouded his eye.

I pocketed the body of his cold dead mate
and hoped, for him, that we weren't too late.
We went in the house to the fireside.
He clutched my finger for the ride.

I placed them both on the hearth of brick;
thinking, to save him, I must be quick.
I went to find him a little feed
and found a package of old bird seed.
But, when I returned, I was too late.
He had fluttered off to join his mate.

The Hero

There is a cross in a Flanders row;
beneath this cross no poppies grow.
A mother, thus, would have it so;
she didn't want her son to go.
So now she grieves her legacy
of a hero's brief insanity.

He was the leader of his group;
they were battalion's go-to troop.

The odds were long with no retreat.
A lobbed grenade fell at their feet.
He heard the warning, "Watch out, Sarge!"
and threw his body on the charge.

For all the medals, pomp, and glory
and the oft-repeated story,
there's still a mother's aching lack:
she'd rather have her soldier back.

City Snow

The snow sits on the city,
a stifling soup of crystal shapes,
blurring the nearby park landscapes.
Darkening the day like just-pulled drapes.

      Tropical animals at the zoo
      wondering what they all should do,
      frightened by this strange new thing
      stepping back from the cold carpeting.

Wondering owners of the stores;
should they be opening up their doors?
For who will venture by this way
on such a late Spring, snowy day?

      Nervous drivers, all uptight,
      wrapped in claustrophobic white.
      Joggers stranded in the park
      listening to the lost dog bark.

Postal walkers on their route;
deliveries will be late, no doubt.
Weathercasters all do say,
the snow won't last another day.

Machu Picchu

The stunning shock of Machu peak.
The Anasazi-like mystique.
Inca spirits in the air,
as though the ghosts still linger there.

The Quechuan whispers amongst the stones,
so skillfully made and carefully laid;
skills that with the skilled did fade.
Walls of stone that terraced soil
and gardens made, with food for all.
Stones reshaped, both large and small,
fitting tight, so waterproof,
no mortar used at all.

Here they lay, masons forgot.
How bodes this for the human lot,
when our stones remain and we do not?

Tree Flag

The flag was torn asunder
by the wind that wrenched it loose;
dragging a piece of frayed-end rope
that held the flag together
before the halyard broke.
A once proud flag, blown afar.
Trapped by a branch of a maple tree,
and held down in ignominy.

There are pieces seen just separately
as the breeze blows leaves aside;
a patch of stripes, a dirty star,
the frayed-end rope, a colored bar.

So from my little balcony
I view this flag quite differently.
For who would kill a stranger
for a piece of striped cloth?
Or salute a sullied, silver star
or pledge allegiance, under God,
to a piece of frayed-end rope?

But when these pieces are together
and unfurled to every breeze
the patriot will do anything
his country's flag to please.

Poem Rainbow

Late afternoon of a throwaway day
my gaze was directed across the way.
A piece of a rainbow hung in the air,
thousands of raindrops held it there.

The sun behind me sent forth its rays:
the drops bent them back, into my gaze.
Each color traveled a different path,
spread thru each drop by refraction math.

More drops transited the curtain bright
bending the rays when their angles were right:
replacing those drops whose job had been done
so the total effect was a constant one.

Rare is the rainbow, full doubly arched,
or the raincloud of such an extent
that all the colors to both arcs are sent,
by properly-sized drops: reflected and bent.
And one arc's order is always reversed;
its color spectrum with the violet first.

There are those who believe and those who pretend
that they know what is there at the rainbow's end.

But I know that they would be searching in vain;
for the only things there are those drops of rain.

Economics

A billion here, a billion there;
a war or two, one here, one there.
Why should anyone still care?

> We borrow billions every day,
> without a thought of how to pay.
> We raise the borrowing bar
> so we can pay the APR.

> We've borrowed such a large amount
> we've lost our economic clout.
> Our children's futures are in doubt
> and former debtors bail us out.

> Seduced again by Greenspan's pitch,
> we give a tax break to the rich.

With funds from FICA tax surplus
we spend it all and hope that, thus,
the economy is stimulated
by this debt that is created.

> It's hard to see where this will end,
> how Fortune will our wealth forfend;
> when they sum the debts of all the bureaus
> and someone asks, "What's that in Euros?"

Memory Shards

I have pointed shards of memory,
that prick through tough denials.
I have shards sharp and beveled,
that slice through tender emotions.

        I have serrated shards of memory
            that saw through hidden hopes.
                I have flattened shards of memory
                   pressing hard my promises.

                  I have dull shards that press gently
                    and call back good old days.
            And there are shards of darkened glass
                    that dimly show my past.

    If only I could put together these scattered shards and see
        that complex, loving person, the one I used to be.

The Predator

The Predator is a weapon
with a television eye
that roams above
the Pashtun sky,
on terrorists to spy.

      Its pilot is in uniform, ten thousand miles away,
      who has to bomb his quota of one terrorist every day.
      No matter that some citizens will be killed along the way,
      they'll just become statistics, collaterally, as they say.

            These citizens are not enemies.
            In fact, they're our allies.
            But the Predator cannot tell this
            from up there in the skies.

So we kill the Pakistani
to stop the Talabani.
This recruits more al Qaeda,
but Obama says "da nada".
If we ever lose this war
they'll come knocking on our door
and kill our people here.

      So we sacrifice our allies
      out of paranoiac fear.
      We're the ostracized pariah,
      everywhere but here.

Stay or Go

When the wine glasses have been emptied
and the candles burned down low,
comes the time for my decision,
should I stay or do I go?

The choice will set the future
for star-crossed path, or no,
I can't wait or hesitate,
do I stay or do I go?

Should I take too long to offer,
then the answer we'll both know.
If I miss the magic moment
I am left with only, go.

Should I choose to linger longer
and hold her hand and say,
"I love you truly, cherie,
should I go or may I stay?"

If she holds my hand with both of hers
and smiles that certain way,
I know I need not question
whether it be go or stay.

But if she stands and says it's late;
that's not a time to hesitate.
This answer means no more debate.
She's showing me the exit gate.

My Dream

A house that seems familiar but somehow not the same.
The rooms are rearranged and reached in different ways.
A few of these are empty, but most are full of things.
In some there are some people, in some I am alone.

A basement full of odds and ends in need of great repairs
I wonder how I got here because there are no stairs.
There's a small door over there but a lion waits outside.
and I know that should he enter, there's no place for me to hide.

Suddenly I am upstairs with people sleeping there.
I cannot find a bed for me and I really do not care.
I'll go outside and drive my car to catch my train or plane,
even though I seem to know I will be late again.

The road is dark, I have no light, I'm racing through the night.
My car is suddenly a toy, not made for all this speed,
but somehow it just seems to be exactly what I need.

Now I'm at the station, waiting for the train.
It comes screeching to a halt, but on the other track.
I'm racing through the tunnel and up the other stair,
but when I reach the platform the train's no longer there.

I'm back within the house again
with awareness seeping in.

My feet on the floor of reality, but things aren't what they seem.
I'm hunting shards of memory in the detritus of a dream.

Three Gorges Dam

On a quiet hill two miles away
I watched Three Gorges Dam that day.
The world's largest, on the Yangtze,
a marvel for tourists to see.
The quiet humming of a turbine wheel,
torqued by water hard as steel,
mass vibrations that I feel.

A water elevator. raising small boats.
and larger locks for all that floats.
The ends of the dam imbeded in rock
since minor shifts cause gates to lock.

Many riparian dwellers displaced
as rising waters their villages erased.
They found compensation for the moving spree
when they learned their electricity was free.
Electric lines radiate over the land
things done with power, no longer by hand.

Stately cruise ships gliding upstream,
elder tourists living a dream.
Clean energy in the extreme.

Afghan Elegy

No kings, chiefs or Mujahedin,
the land is ruled by hands unseen.
Silk-laden camels *ungulating* west
at ghostlike oases no longer rest.

Nomadic tents now dot the land,
simple structures, made by hand.
Nighttime winds move ancient sand.

Chewing camels' shadows lengthen,
huddling up as cool winds strengthen;
moaning through the mountain passes
revealing hidden desert caches,
left from numerous futile clashes
of forces foreign and internal
that were seeking peace eternal.

Neither U.S. nor al Qaeda,
bin Laden or Taliban,
No dire shadow from a drone,
no Stinger missile boom.

Only poppy fields in bloom,
underneath a Pashtun moon.

Stuck Song

Did you ever have a song
stuck in your head
that didn't go away
when you climbed into bed?

Just when it's complete,
it starts to repeat,
only now its tempo
is a different beat.

It starts out in C,
then slides into B,
then right after that
it shifts to B-flat.
And just for a tease
it runs a reprise.

And right when you're able
to adjust to the theme
you drift off to sleep
and it's there in your dream.

Love

Our bonds keep us apart when together,
and together when apart.
Our love keeps passion on a tether
and lives in one another's heart.

With fondness honed by absence
and sad separating sweet,
our love must work to find a way
so we can love another day.

Our love is solace for each other
lying quiet through the day,
then rising up to help recover
our needy spirits on the way.

Our love is unrequited,
though the coals of passion glow.
Soon our love may be ignited
though its rising might be slow.
Then our souls would be united
in peace that only lovers know.

But time defeats the restless heart,
and passes, like a gliding dove,
as passion's embers slowly cool
to silent cinders of hopeless love.

Cormorants

Heading southward past my floor
every morning, to explore.
What they find, I can't be sure.
Wings extended, feathers aflair,
beaks protruding pierce the air.
Going forth, I know not where,
but for hours they'll be out there.

To return afternoon,
gliding homeward past my place,
soaring by with awkward grace
pretending that it's not a race.

Surfing unseen waves of air,
competing with a no-flap dare:
to hold a glide 'till they are there.
Sailing by without a care
home with daylight hours to spare.

Savoir Faire

Trois old frenchmen dans le Paris
un jour en parc these words did dit,
"Of savoir faire what do we know?".
"What do you say, Monsieur Beau?"

I say if you come home,
early afternoon, unknown,
to find your wife in bed upstairs
with par amour and unawares;
you carefully close the door and leave,
saying softly, s'il vous please,
treading gently down the stair.
Ca, pour moi, c'est savoir faire.

Mais non, ami, though what you say is true.
You must first add, said number two,
a word to let them know you're there.
I would say "continuez",
and let them think I really care;
that I'm the one with savoir faire.

Le troisieme homme does, nodding, say
what you have said is very vrai.
But for me to say "continuez",
must sound to them just like a dare.
If then they can, with bodies bare,
then they're the ones with savoir faire.

Fade To Black

What I expect is simply this,
when life my cells do lack,
they all will stop their work
and fade away to black.

I came from black, cell by cell,
and in due time, a baby well.
From there, with cells having their way,
I'm a human being, here today.

How cells understand
what they have to do
is still a mystery to me and you.

But the pattern is there
for the cells to share
and they just know
when to go and where.

But to say at some point,
that a person is there,
is to be more certain than I care to dare.

But when we die, of this I'm sure,
it's fade to black and shut the door.

I Am A Dog

I am a dog.
I shake myself dry.
I lose all the wet
on the very first try.

I am a dog
with a great sense of smell.
Whose tracks I am following
I always can tell.

I'm a dog in the park,
even though it be dark,
I can tell where they went
by their lingering scent.

I am a dog on your lap,
we both are content
and for comforting you
is why I've been sent.

I'm a dog on a buzz
running circles around
as this speedy dog does
with four-on-the-ground.

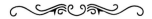

Poem Kitchen

Black stove crouched at the chimney,
the soul of a country kitchen,
consuming crafted pieces of wood
raising heat to its warming hood.

           Detachable flatirons in a heated niche
           water reservoir heated, filled and ready.
           Warm air from the oven door
           and fresh-swept ashes on the floor.

An anxious cook her bread dough kneads
thinking of the mouths to feed.
Pots and pans, a need to fill,
await her skill on the black stove grill.
Potatoes for the oven, hunger pangs to still.

           Perched upon her thinking stool:
           children coming home from school
           need to keep them occupied
           with new ideas, yet untried.

           Six settings, snacks to share,
           eight chairs around table square
           unassigned but dedicated
           by words unspoken, yet understood,
           like cows knowing their place in the barn.

A snack of grapes, a piece of cheese,
a piece of bread buttered with ease.
A glass of milk from the morning's chores
topped off with dessert smores.

A reading from "Five Little Peppers",
story of a family like ours.
Soon the father will be home
from building county roads.

Girls, giggling, hugging, kissing
and the boys with high-fives,
their dad with tears in eyes.
Mom, feeling the love power,
knowing this be the family hour.

In Memoriam

Each year we set aside a day
to remember as we pray
for those who with their lives did pay,
for our freedom, so they say.

But what does freedom have to fear,
unless the enemies come here?
It seems to me, a logic rare,
to always fight their war out there.

We fight the war to win the peace
as though we think the wars will cease;
but coming from the distant past,
as in countless times before,
we hear the senseless drums of war.

We worship those who give their sons
to die on nameless soil
but would we give so willingly
were it our turn to toil?

The Poets' Hour

However dark and late at night
when I feel the urge to write,
thinking of a line so bright,
I rise and reach out for the light.

When cares and fears recede
and sleep no longer is a need,
I stop to meditate
and long again to just create.

Then quiet lures the word to power
and brings to past the poets' hour.

To thoughts sublime my mind will race
but words come forth at their own pace.

All with such passion, love and grace
never an iamb lost to waste.

Democracy

There's a thing that's called democracy
that's not what it's supposed to be.
It should be only people's rule,
at least that's what we're taught in school.

We have to have elections
to determine what corrections
must be made in our directions
toward socialist infections.

It's based on a constitution
that's a written resolution
that defines an institution
for government by consent
of people happy and content.

But half the people here are not
consenting now to what we've got.
If you have a Cuban government
it is proportional involvement
of all who send a represent.

The conference picks a president
and every one can have a say
and not restrained to just one day.

Of course, that's not democracy
when people get to have their say
and power doesn't have its way.

To equate democracy with capitalism
and freedom with free marketing
means our leaders have the liberty
to exploit us all deliberately.

What of the people who do not vote,
whose needs are not addressed?
Does democracy work for them
or are they dispossessed?

And when the highest court decides
and ballot problems overrides;
can we still say that this provides
Democracy for different sides?
Or then no longer can we say
we have Democracy today.

Hands

Hands that only want to heal,
skillful with the surgeon's steel.
Hands that with gentle massage
relief of tensions do presage.
Hands that soothing salve apply,
telling children not to cry.

Hands that heartbeats do restore,
help with breathing and much more.
Hands that wring in brief despair,
hands that fold in silent prayer.
Hands that mold the softened clay
or sometimes chip the stone away.

Many hands together moving
making music as they're proving
that they're following commands
from their guest conductor's hands.

Hands that hold the artist's brush,
and paint the pastel sunset's blush.
Hands that show their might
by the words they write.

Hands that serious games do play,
pleasing fans who choose to pay.
Hands that labor every day,
creating wealth along their way.

Pro Basketball

There's this game called basketball,
played by men who are very tall.
They run up and down the floor,
taking turns trying to score.

Bouncing while running is called a dribble,
if the ref calls traveling, do not quibble.
With teeth clenched tight and visage grim,
they slam a dunk and swing from the rim.

With a secret signal for an alley-oop
the catcher soars and stuffs the hoop.
With tricky footwork and a body fake
the dribbler spins, for a drive to make.

A pass outside to the open man
who'll make a swisher, if he can.
A rush backcourt to stop a fast break,
with luck it's two points the others don't make.

The game has changed in many ways
since I played in olden days.
The rules now favor the larger man
and encourage scoring to please the fan.

I suggest some changes to the rules,
to be enforced at all the schools.
Put the rim at fifteen feet
to allow the short man to compete.
Subtract a point for every miss
and add a point for every swish.
Let defenders tackle the man with the ball
and stop talking trash at the referee's call.

Jacaranda

He stood atop the modern inn
with panoramic view,
and gazed upon Wilshire below
now lined with brilliant hue.

How they would have marveled
to see that building rise,
against the desert skies,
glass-curtained, tinted, multi-roomed;
when Autochthon met the Spaniard
and the jacarandas bloomed.

He walked the scented streets below
past carport, house and pool
and remembering desert heritage,
realized why the air was cool.

Where saguaro cacti once did grow
now condominiums loom:
and just like soldiers, row on row,
the jacarandas bloom.

Now, time has passed, he sits alone,
his friends have gone their way
and memories do his vision save
of a distant, sunny May;
where once, their branches bare,
with flowers plumed,
the jacarandas bloomed.

We

The way we were, yesterday,
the way we are, today.
It doesn't make much sense to me
though I'm hearing what you say.

I feel a distance creeping in
and it would surely be a sin
to let it stay another day
and not to make it go away.

Am I not the same?
Your helpful friend in need.
Your patient listener, who your request
does almost always heed?

What change you see,
I do not know;
and not understanding
I must seem very slow.

Is it that often I forget
and say some things I should regret
or fail to say the thoughtful word
to let you know my heart's been stirred?

What will tomorrow say to me
about the way it used to be?
I guess I'll have to wait and see
whether it be You and I, or We.
for You and I it's separate ways,
while We can look to happy days.

The Path To Terrorism

It started in Afghanistan,
the CIA had made a plan
to be there when the Russians ran
and help install the Taliban.

With missiles to Mujahideen,
we invited them to join our team.
They became our staunchest covert friends,
selling Stingers for their own ends.

Osama came and built his camps
and trained recruits to light the lamps
of terrorism in the lands
that ring the Middle Eastern sands.

Our President declared a war
against this man he deemed a poor
example of a terror lord
who lead a rag-tag terror horde.

He said we'll have him, alive or dead,
and put a price upon his head,
but invaded Afghanistan instead.
He put Karzai in Kabul
and forgot bin Laden, like a fool.

But yet another group arose
our hegemony they would oppose
They would call themselves Al Qaeda men
and soon our safety they'd offend.

They trained some pilots to fly our planes
and sent our buildings down in flames.

This terrorism called for war
and, not knowing what could be in store,
Bush planned to change Saddam's regime
and replace it with Alawai's team.

There were no Dubyayou MD's
but Congress thought they should appease
a President that longed for war,
so that's what they all voted for.

It started with great shock and awe,
just possibly against the law,
but the justices did consent
and sanctified the President.

Though Saddam now is history,
our getting out's a mystery.
The world has come to know our shame,
for terrorism we're to blame.

Dark Park

One night in the very dark
I took a shortcut through the park.
The denizens of the night were there,
each hiding in a private lair.

> Some, wrapped in blankets, full asleep
> had prayed the Lord their souls to keep.
> Others flittered here and there
> and jumped at me and tried to scare.

> A peacock screaming up above
> told me he was not a dove.

> A garden snake by day
> was a python, slithering away.

> A squirrel climbing up a tree
> sounded like a tiger cat to me.

I trudged determinedly ahead,
looking foward to my bed,
knowing; save for lucky breaks,
I'd be sleeping here instead.

I, Bichon

I'm Bichon Frise, bred to please.
Give me a chore and I'll do more.
I greet with gusto most everyone,
so many, my job is never done.

Grunting and speeding, I do a buzz
like all bichons do, and just because.

Lying on laps is a specialty,
particularly if they're petting me;
or brushing my coat with a gentle stroke.

When they rub my tummy, it feels so yummy,
that I settle down for a longer stay,
but then they decide that I'm in their way.
I'm really gentle with a small girl or boy
and I let them play fetch with my special toy.

My favorite joy is a walk in the park
where saucy squirrels give me reason to bark.
The Canada geese waddle and squawk,
I ignore them all and strut my walk.

Later it's dinner and maybe a treat,
it's usually a chew, but never a sweet.
Another outdoors after I'm fed
then it's time to jump onto their bed.

Crusades

On the one road to Baghdad
(the worst trip I ever had)
stood a billboard, worn and tattered,
by the war it had been shattered.

Still, some words there could be read,
and this is what those words said;
this is a crusade scoreboard, Yankee hero,
it says "Muslims one and Christians zero."

As I drove along and pondered,
to a new thought my mind wandered;
had not history with its sight
proved that neither could be right?
Still they want to start a fight
to demonstrate religious might.

In the darkness of that night,
I finally saw the "knowing" light.
Others wonder what is right,
when and where to join the fight.
But I am sure, after that night,
that we should think before we fight.

Grandpa

Greyhound station in Wilkes-Barre
younger brother in my care.
Take him to Gomer's farm.
Make sure he doesn't come to harm.

From Jersey up to Gouverneur
change in Pennsylvania,
all night bus ride,
grab some sleep.

Aunt Bernice's letter said
just one boy for the summer.
Mom selected brother George,
he not yet used to urban life.

I would rather roam Manhattan,
I'd had enough of farmer life.
After this trip the summer's mine,
though I might find a city job.

The bus is loading,
tickets behind the driver.
On the aisle I can see the road,
pretend I'm driving as I doze.

Morning finds us leaving bus
wait for Bernice to come for us.
Here's Gramps address
try to stop and say hello.

Which way to Elm street;
now who'd be there, the lady asks.
It's my grandpa Carr.
A man said I'll take you thar.

We found him on his porch
slowly rocking as he read.
Your boys are here, man leaving said;
book down he squinted as we stood.

His wisp of hair was whiteish gray
his blue eyes held us both at bay.
I scarcely heard him softly say
You'd be Ada's boys, he said.

My thought was mean, he was so old
who might it be instead?
Brown spots on his face and hands
I never want to be that old.

We got acquainted, sat and talked;
he told us of mother as a girl.
A neighbor brought him breakfast
saying Mabel will bring your lunch.

You've both been up all night
you need ice cream all right.
They knew him at the store;
proudly he watched and made sure

that all there knew his role
in our visit to the town.
Then on to Greyhound's elegance
To wait the ride to Gomer's farm.

We slept and ate, left George there.
Back to the bus, headed home.
I had some more time left to spare
and there was Grandpa in his chair.

Tell me more how it was
when Mom and Dad first met.
He put his old hand on my arm
saying please don't leave me yet.

I felt strange being there with him
but told my self it was okay.
He's Grandpa, I'm grandson,
it should always be that way.

You travel on a wonder bus
not invented in my day.
It was horse and harness with a shay
and grain and hay, I heard him say.

We sat and talked as darkness came
He seemed proud to play his role
to tell of long ago
I felt a strange, unwanted bond.

Could I ever play that role?
Could I make a young boy feel proud
to know me, share my journey;
could I even be a grandson.

I'm glad you had some time to spend.
Tell Ada I love her.
You better run
It's time for your bus.

I knew the streets
running fast to the bus.
You needn't have run,
I was holding the bus for you.

Later on the bus alone
I thought of neighbors helping him.
The kindness of strangers,
or were they?
just a community.

How to explain to mom
that gramps and me are friends.
I think she'll understand,
he is her dad, you know.

By Your Leave

They say that we must have a plan
a plan that tells how we will leave.
A plan to pull the troops back home.
The best our generals can conceive.

Instead of dates we'll have events
that, when finished, we believe
will allow us to reduce the force
and bring some more troops home, of course.

We'll train and train Iraqi troops
until they have enough divisions
that they can make their own decisions
though we'll provide them with provisions.

We'll find some other tasks to add to justify our staying,
and help them output some more oil so for our stay their paying.
They'll need our help on their committees as we Haliburtonize their cities.
Power and water we'll provide to win them over to our side.

Then roads will come and oil pipes too
there's oh so much that we can do.
We will need to build a base or two
to house the troops that'll oversee
and protect their demiraqcracy.
Then we will stay 'till they believe
that we don't plan to ever leave.

My Brother

He was ever my brother,
but I knew him not.
Our lifelines parallel,
close not our lot.

Time carried us both
to our writing days,
each penning our thoughts
in our separate ways.

Then life gave us time
to be together.
A few days we had
to do whatever.

Now I know all the things
he did with his time,
Days just as important
as any of mine.

For many do toil
for the wealth of a few,
but the salt of the earth
will carry us through.

Trees

I stopped to see a tree,
because it spoke to me.
I knew it said we're brothers
cause we're both made up of cells.
I said, but your cells are different,
they're not the same as mine.

> A breeze ruffled the tree's leaves
> and I felt it blow my hair.
> You see, he said, we feel the same wind
> as it's blowing in our hair.
> My cells are bark and yours are skin
> and yours let moisture out
> and mine let moisture in.
> Oh, sure, he said, there're some differences
> but when we add them all together
> we are closer to each other
> than we are; whatever.

I said, your roots will bind you
you can never move about.
He said I have all I need right here
so travel I can do without.
My sap runs down into my roots
and stays there in the cold.

> I can stay here in the winter's worst
> and know my pipes will never burst.
> But you would freeze, your cells would die
> beneath the ground you'd be forced to lie.

I said that I would go inside
and put on clothes before I died.
I'd stand before my fireplace
and feel the warmth upon my face
from heat that came from burning wood.

He said, of course you could,
but that would cost you all the good
of having trees give oxygen
and absorbing all the CO_2
that into the air you humans spew.

My leaves can photosynthesize
so saving me would be quite wise.
I left him there to find a drink
and now I know that trees can think.

The Iceberg

The ship has hit the iceberg, the global has beem warmed.
The deck chairs lined up in a row,
the lifeboat line is formed.
Tornadoes are more frequent, floods and drought abound
Earthquakes and tsunamis
are scattered all around.

All those who could be helpful resist Al Gore sell.
Before we give up profits, we'll see you all in Hell.
The auto makers all agree, their task is MPG.
They know that this is not enough, but asked for more, they'll just hang tough.

The power companies burn coal, less imported oil their goal.
They know pollution has its toll,
but making profit is their role.

For all others, bene nota, there exists a carbon quota.
Too little, much too late and tragic, we all must wait for skeptics' magic.

The Tipping Point is not yet here;
though those liberals think it's near.
Cut the trees, drive SUV's
And move away from rising seas.

The Road

The road to Hell is paved
with good intentions, so they say.
With spaced guard-rails of shattered dreams,
anchored along the way.

Its ditches littered with debris,
the detritus of unreal hopes;
a price we all must pay.

Its berms are pocked with little fears
and pools of paranoia;
hidden from the view of years
by rows and rows of hoya.

Some road signs point the other way
and some say do not enter
and one in fancy Latin's there
to caveat the emptor.

There are no exits here today.
If you start you must continue
on your journey all the way.

If you stop and shift into reverse,
there will just be Hell to pay.

P.T.S.S.

Home from Afghanistan,
looking for the other man.
His friends would really like to see
that happy guy he used to be.

His restless sleep is made of dreams
filled with his wounded buddy's screams,
with turbaned shadows in the night
erupting in a fire fight.

He hopes that those who sent him there
will let him know that they still care,
by approving the syndrome's support needs;
created by his stressful deeds.

Flash to the truck in front of him
twenty men and a truck blown apart.
How do they know which truck to blow,
could there be spies or are they that smart.

What if the signal were delayed
and my truck was the price we paid.
Survivor guilt has you dismayed
but you were dealt the hand you played.

Last night it was the Medevac
a chopper carrying wounded friends.
An RPG and a ball of flame
a horrible sight as the nightmare ends.

A loyal bus boy in the mess hall, wanting his family to save from certain Shiite retribution, accepts the body bomb solution.

When the war is finally over
and for others the fighting's done,
the soldier with the syndrome
relives the war at home.

About Me

It was never about me,
what I wanted to be.
It was how does that play for the family.
Then one day I left, for myself I enlisted,
and the temptation to return
I have always resisted.

It might have been better
had I stayed in my rut
but the feeling to wander
still lives in my gut.

The lands I have seen
and the places I've been
have taught me so much
of the troubles of men.

Today I am wiser,
I've put down some roots.
I've hung out my shingle
and hung up my boots.

I no longer live in a restless mode;
I'm happy in my humble abode.
I still watch the contrails, high overhead,
but tell myself; watch the horizon instead.
But if places to travel I'm allowed to rank,
I'd wake up tomorrow in the Paris *George Cinq*.

Rain

Rain, sometimes fine and gentle,
falling softly,
recycling water,
washing off dust.

Sometimes torrential,
flooding, eroding,
causing damage,
making news.

Sometimes denying,
evaporating in air,
leaving the earth
arid and bare.

Sometimes harsh,
a horizontal sheet,
flattening crops,
corn and wheat.

Sometimes absent
for too long a time
leaving earth so very dry,
that irrigation is the cry.

Sometimes with sunshine all aglow,
arching the sky
in a wonderful bow.

Night Snow

Standing near windows by night,
looking at the nearest light,
I watched a snow replace the sleet
and cover up the icy street.

Sifting through the cone of light,
quietly falling through the night,
tossed by the wind to left and right
the tiny crystals filled my sight.

Delicate patterns for all to see,
obeying crystallography.

Coming to rest after their labors;
arranging themselves
as close-packed neighbors.

Covering all that I could see,
a gift of nature, just for me.
Resting where they want to be,
a subject for photography.

Life

Small gains, in life, come slowly
the worst of losses, come so fast.
The face of fate can whip around
from charming smile to dour frown.
For all our planning for the worst,
it seems to always happen first.

As fortunes fade and bubbles burst
we find our treasures have been cursed.
Our luck turns downward for a spell,
misfortune comes to wish us well.
Disaster strikes us at the bell
and life becomes a living hell.

And yet, for some, with no good reason,
their karma seems to know no season.
For every day's their lucky day,
and their one-armed bandits always pay.

My guardian angel has no wings,
he sits in contemplation.
When I ask him why this is
he frowns in indignation.

He thinks probably it is my fate,
to be unlucky, and I should wait.
My turn will come some later date.
Ideas like that I really hate.

Hope

Hope is the elusive ingredient of Faith
that sees the unseen.
Hope is the pilot-light of the flame
Resolve.
Hope is a fountain, running deep,
flowing with promises to keep.

Hope, leavening a mothers love,
is the rebar of life's concrete.
Hope dissolves despair,
giving courage to life's trials bear.
The will of Hope must be strong
lest gambling be Hope gone wrong.

Whatever architecture there may be,
Hope is the structure we don't see.
Carrying us over our daily woes,
lighting the candle of strength that glows.

Birds of a Feather

A Cassowary is quite scary,
but an osterich he's not.
They're genetically related,
for some genes were once conflated.
I think it's really very cool
that once they shared the same gene pool.

This by Mendelian rule,
which we learned about in school,
would seem to make them cousins
and relate them by the dozens.

There may have been a Cassorich,
hiding in a gene pool niche;
or perhaps an ostewary
lurking in the commissary.
The possibilities are quite hairy,
and we can't afford to tarry
with the work that we should do
to return these creatures to the zoo.

We'll put them with a ratite
and hope that they won't fight.
If we only had an emu
things would surely be alright.
I'm sure by now you have no doubt
and know what this flap's all about.

Winter Snow

Tiny crystals in the air
falling down on city square,
making sparkles in my hair
and covering clothing that I wear.

Landing softly on my face,
melting bits of icy lace.
Coming down they seem so bold,
but once they melt they're not so cold.

Going any place they dare
covering earth that once was bare,
sifting down just everywhere
and making winter scenes so rare.

Yes, it's snowing. Is that fair?
Maybe not, but I don't care,
I'll just snuggle in my lair
and they won't find me hiding there.

Woman

Sometimes thinking thoughts out loud,
sometimes her quiet head is bowed,
wreathed in silken halo blond,
thinking images so fond.
Ministering to all around,
sharing knowledge that she's found,
helping others on their way,
filling up her mitzvah day.

She's often quite gregarious,
turns to strangers, leaving us.
She finds the best in everyone
and talking to them is such fun.
Can she be so innocent,
is that what she really meant?
But knowing how her thoughts are pure,
of her intent one can be sure.

Self-conflicted by her past,
trying bad days to outlast,
remembering stress to nerves so tender
of life's thrusts that did offend her.

Talking now of happy ways,
thinking back to lighter days
managing her real estate,
should she move or should she wait?
Maybe at a later date,
she might find a better rate.

Her doctor's MRI reveals
the inner trauma she conceals
by suppressing all the fears
that she can't lose by shedding tears.

Shattered hope on shattered hope,
she can manage still to cope.
Wondering if her message clear
will fall again on deafened ear.

Anchored to religious base
at her monastery place
with her joy upon her face
from her happy inner grace.

Air

As humans we should take more care
of this substance we call AIR.
It protects us from attacks from space
by meteors, asteroids and particles
that otherwise are articles
that would destroy all signs of life.

Air is made of many things
but mostly nitrogen and oxygen.
All forms of life need oxygen
and air provides it where and when.

Air gives us clouds and rain
that many forms of life sustain.
It spreads the sunshine all around
and keeps earth green, instead of brown.

We hurt the air when we pollute,
as off to work we all commute.
Industrially plumes of waste are forming,
as we blame the air for warming.

We build those windmills everywhere,
taking energy from the air
and we think the air can still
all its other roles fulfill.

Air helps our planes to fly each day
the unseen lanes of the skyway
and dissipates the jet exhaust,
another breath of air is lost.

Tai Chi

Early morning they all meet
in the park the sun to greet.
The Park provides the lessons free
so folks can learn about Tai Chi.

The moves are ancient,
and they're traditional.
When slowly done,
they're physically conditional.

It's exercise for seniors too
and all the movements they can do.
And if they should forget the sequence
no one notices a short pretense.

Each movement has a name
that gives the move its claim to fame.
When warding off and push do fail,
there's always grasp the sparrow's tail.

Abundance of Canada geese
wondering warily about these
creatures and what they do.
Swooping swallows wonder too.

Golden dome just above treetop
with a Rocky Mountain backdrop.
City towers in a vapor
like a color print on paper.

Slim

A thousand head of restless steers,
a thousand miles of trail.
My cowboys will deliver them
and put them up for sale.

A shimmering, dusty wave of heat,
creating a mirage.
The cattle do not realize
it's Nature's camouflage.

They think it's a pool of water,
their thirst will drive their need.
One steer begins to run
and starts a wild stampede.

Of all the dangers cowboys face,
the worst is a stampede.
But my cowboys, knowing all the risks,
are competing for the lead.

The lead must break their forward speed
and turn them in a circle track.
They'll mill around and quiet down
and become a docile pack.

And through the dusty, murky cloud,
the lead man's working with a whip.
It's cowboy Slim, his face is grim.
He hopes his pony doesn't slip.

A gopher hole, a broken leg,
the worst, as we all feared.
And we all felt a pang of grief
as Slim and pony disappeared.

A hundred heavy, pounding hooves
would seal the cowboy's fate.
We all went back to find our mate,
though we all knew we'd be too late.

We buried Slim where he did lie,
underneath the prairie sky.
We bowed our heads, prayed a prayer,
said goodbye and left him there.

We finally made the trail's end,
delivering all the steers.
Then, thinking back to Slim's bravery,
we all gave him three cheers.

Some of the money from the steers
we divvied up amongst Slim's peers.
There's enough for all, but none to spare
so we made sure Slim had a share.

Then we headed for the town saloon,
planning toasts for Slim.
Knowing, with some certainity,
the drinks would be on him.

City Park

Tree shadows covering the ground,
Squirels hurrying all around.
Pedal boats on the lake
Fast enough to leave a wake.

Empty see-saws in the rain
wait for children's weight in vain.
The air will dry the dripping rings;
the sun will dry the other things.

Glistening in the morning sun,
promising hours of youthful fun.
Silent pipes, the swings and rings,
absent all the children's things.

Groups of geese eating grass,
waiting for the day to pass.
A sudden rush to fly instead,
barely missing someone's head.

A bunch of people with a tree,
what will their purpose prove to be?
Are they stealing city loot
or is it just a photo-shoot.

Weekly concert at the shell,
music that the crowd knows well.
People standing in a queue,
waiting for the porta-loo.

Distant noises from the zoo,
peacocks, tigers, lions, too
blended with the local hum
adding to a pleasant sum.

Ski Snow

Powder on powder; skier's delight,
falling softly thru the night.
Moving on at morning light,
leaving slopes glistening white.

Snow-capped gondolas
all on a string.
The summit awaits
the guests they will bring.

After a coffee; the first thrilling run.
A downward schuss; exhilerating fun.
Early on, by shadowless light.
Like an eagle's flight, beating the sun.

All thru the day
the endless queues
of people with skis
the slopes will abuse.

At the end of the day
the skis go away.
The snow crystals broken
and crushed where they lay.

Planetrise

How common is the sunrise
and the looming of the moon
but rarely seen by casual eyes,
the special sight of planetrise.

The subtle creep of horizon chord
across the bright sunrising pie
brings slowly forth the full-grown orb
that lights the Eastern sky.

Subtle not is the planetrise,
a sudden strike to waiting eyes;
from just not there to being there
a steady spark piercing the air.

Not certain like the moon or sun
to say its journey has began.
It could be just an aircraft light
punching through the murk of night.

But when slowly moving up the arc,
that knowing eyes sketch in the dark,
each moment makes for certain, more;
that it's a planetrise for sure.

The Service

To celebrate, memorialize; for closure,
of a life that touched them all.
The coffin at the altar,
the priest, fussing with his shawl.

Twelve colored glass panes,
their icons looking down;
eerily lighting up the hall.
Windows to another place,
issuing a commanding call.

Stain-glass haloes worn by all,
seemingly same sized haloes;
be the wearer large or small.

Different colors signify
an hierarchy for the eye.
Are the pictured angels ranked
like people when they die?

The priest reads the twenty-third
though they all join in, he still is heard;
The traveler's journey is assured.
Our Father follows, word for word.
Silence follows for a while,
people thinking what's occurred.

The incense burner is held in sway,
the pungent cloud rises away
and ends the service for the day;
the blessed traveler's on his way.

Deja Vu

I feel I'm standing next to you,
I know it's only deja vu.
I feel your presence, very near
If only you were really here.

We said goodbye, each went our way,
hoping we'd be back some day.
There's something here,
but it's not you.
It's just another deja vu.

Sometimes a dream seems very real,
stirring thoughts I often feel,
remembering times I spent with you
and I awake to deja vu.

Friends tell me that I look blue
and they ask me,
"What's with you?"
I have to tell them,
'cause it's true,
Our love was only deja vu.